Y

D0914722

WITHDRAWN

WONDER WOMAN™ MYTHOLOGY

Wonder Woman and the Monsters of Myth

by STEVE KORTÉ

Wonder Woman created by William Moulton Marston

Consultant:
Laurel Bowman
Department of Greek and Roman Studies
University of Victoria
British Columbia, Canada

CAPSTONE PRESS
a capstone imprint

Published by Capstone Press in 2017
1710 Roe Crest Drive
North Mankato, Minnesota 56003
www.mycapstone.com

STAR37672

Library of Congress Cataloging-in-Publication Data is available on
the Library of Congress website.

ISBN: 978-1-5157-4583-9 (library binding)
ISBN: 978-1-5157-4596-9 (eBook PDF)

Summary: Introduces a variety of creatures and monsters from
Greek, Roman, African, and other world mythologies, and explores
how they are woven into the fabric of Wonder Woman's backstory.

Editor: Christopher Harbo

Designer: Tracy McCabe

Creative Director: Bob Lentz

Production Specialist: Katy LaVigne

Image Credits:
Capstone Press: Stefano Azzalin, 15, Daniel Ferran, 23, Estudio
Haus, 7, 13, Nadine Takvorian, 11, 16, Scott Altmann, 8, 26;
Dreamstime: Linda Bucklin, cover (bottom left and top left);
iStockphoto: Grafissimo, cover, (bottom right); Shutterstock:
Barashkova Natalia, 28, Drpixel, 7 (inset), Everett Historical, 21,
Foxyliam, 19 (inset), Kazakova Maryia, 20, MarcusVDT, 17 (inset),
paul prescott, 29, Pres Panayotov, 12, sebartz, 27, Sergey Mikhaylov,
24, Vuk Kostic, 19, Vuk Kostic, cover, (top right); Warner Brothers,
throughout (Wonder Woman and backgrounds)

Printed and bound in the USA.
010061S17

TABLE OF CONTENTS

Myths, Monsters, and a Mighty Amazon

Myths are famous stories, and the story of Wonder Woman is one of the most famous of all. Before she became a world-renowned super hero, she was Princess Diana. She grew up on a hidden island called Themyscira, and she came from a line of brave women known as the Amazons. These **immortals** lived together peacefully, far from the rest of the world. Occasionally, however, evildoers surfaced on their island — including rampaging monsters. Many of the monsters were imprisoned in a series of tunnels behind Doom's Doorway, a sealed door on the island.

When she became a young woman, Diana journeyed from Themyscira on a mission to fight evil in "man's world," as the Amazons called it. Now known as Wonder Woman, she bravely battled hundreds of deadly monsters. Some of these creatures were newly escaped from the dark tunnels below Doom's Doorway. Most of them were made famous in centuries-old mythological tales.

Get ready to join Wonder Woman as she uses her amazing Amazon powers to fight these terrifying creatures. You may be surprised by how many of her fearsome foes come from the classic world of myth.

immortal—someone who is able to live forever

CHAPTER 1
Angry Giants

CYCLOPS

In Greek mythology, the goddess Gaia gave birth to the Cyclops siblings. These one-eyed giants were larger than the tallest oak trees. They labored as blacksmiths and supplied weapons to the gods. Some of the weapons included thunderbolts for Zeus, a trident for Poseidon, and a helmet of invisibility for Hades.

The Cyclops known as Polyphemus once fell in love with the sea-nymph Galatea. But she was in love with a young shepherd named Acis instead. In a jealous rage, Polyphemus crushed Acis with a boulder and killed him. After the Cyclops fled to a faraway cave, Galatea transformed Acis into a flowing river so that he could always be near her.

The Greek poet Homer described the Cyclopes as savage creatures that lived within caves on an island. When the great warrior Odysseus sailed his fleet of ships too close to the Cyclopes' island, Polyphemus ate six of Odysseus' sailors! To fight back, Odysseus plunged a sharpened stick into the giant's one eye, blinding him forever.

Wonder Woman first battled Polyphemus when he escaped from the underworld of dead souls known as Hades. Polyphemus and his two brothers had been **banished** to Hades' lowest level — the pits of Tartarus. While trapped in that horrible place, Polyphemus ate his siblings! Wonder Woman defeated Polyphemus when he invaded the Amazon's home island of Themyscira. She banished him once again to the depths of Tartarus.

banish—to send away forever

WHY ONE EYE?

The legend of Cyclopes having only one eye may be based on the work habits of ancient blacksmiths. They often wore an eye patch over one eye to prevent injury from flying sparks. If a spark blinded the unprotected eye, the blacksmith would still have one good eye to work with.

FACT

More than 400 species of freshwater one-eyed crustaceans are known as Cyclopes. Unlike the mythological Cyclopes, they are tiny. Some are smaller than 1/100 of an inch long.

COTTUS

In addition to giving birth to the Cyclops siblings, the Greek goddess Gaia also gave birth to the Hecatoncheires. These three giant beasts were named Cottus, Briareus, and Gyges. Each of them had 50 heads and 100 arms, and they were all incredibly stupid. Despite their lack of intelligence, they were feared because of their terrible tempers and superhuman strength. Some said that Cottus toppled a mountain by throwing heavy boulders at it. Uranus, the father of Cottus, was so disgusted by his children that he banished them to the pits of Tartarus. There they stayed for more than 2,000 years.

During their time in Tartarus, a war broke out among the gods that almost destroyed the universe. The god Zeus chose to free Cottus and his brothers, and won the war. Their freedom was short-lived, though. Zeus soon sent them back to Tartarus and gave them the job of guarding the losers of the war. Cottus and his siblings were so stupid that they thought this was a great honor.

In the world of Wonder Woman, the Amazons guarded Doom's Doorway. This sealed portal led to some of the world's most ferocious monsters, including Cottus. The first **mortal** to visit Themyscira was an American test pilot named Diana Trevor. Shortly after her arrival, Cottus smashed through Doom's Doorway. Diana Trevor bravely fought the beast and saved the Amazons. Years later, her name would be given in honor to Princess Diana, the most famous Amazon of all.

mortal—human, referring to a being who will eventually die

CHAPTER 2
Beastly Creatures

CERBERUS

In Greek and Roman myth, Cerberus was a giant hound that prowled the gates of Hades. The ferocious three-headed watchdog guarded the entrance, displaying razor-sharp teeth and dripping poisonous foam from his mouth. He only stepped aside to allow a new dead soul to enter the underworld. Cerberus also made sure that no dead souls could ever escape Hades.

One man was brave enough to try to tame Cerberus. His name was Orpheus, and he was the most famous musician in Greece. After his wife, Eurydice, was killed by a snakebite, Orpheus traveled to Hades to bring her back to life. When he arrived at the gates, he played his **lyre** so beautifully and sang so movingly that Cerberus wagged his tail like a puppy. He let Orpheus enter.

Wonder Woman journeyed several times to the underworld of dead souls. Each time, she confronted Cerberus. Their most unusual encounter happened during an annual contest on Themyscira. Diana's mother dropped a golden apple into the depths of Hades and challenged her daughter to prevent it from hitting the ground. Cerberus caught the apple in his mouth. Just as he was about to drop it at the feet of his master, Wonder Woman inhaled her breath with hurricane force, causing the apple to fly to her.

lyre—a small, stringed, harplike instrument played
mostly in ancient Egypt, Israel, and Greece

MINOTAUR

The Minotaur was a fierce monster in Greek mythology with the head of a bull and the body of a man. The Minotaur was born of a fire-breathing bull and Queen Pasiphaë, who was the wife of King Minos of Crete. King Minos imprisoned the Minotaur within the Labyrinth, a building filled with hundreds of tunnels that offered no escape. Each year, the king sent 14 young Athenians into the Labyrinth as a **sacrifice** to the Minotaur. They were never seen again.

One man was brave enough to enter the Labyrinth and fight the Minotaur. He was Prince Theseus of Athens. The king's daughter, Ariadne, was in love with Theseus, and gave him a ball of thread and a sword. He unraveled the thread as he made his way through the Labyrinth's winding corridors. Then he killed the Minotaur with the sword and followed the thread back out of the Labyrinth.

Princess Diana was a fierce warrior, but she also tried to control her mighty powers and show mercy. When she was a young girl, she fought a Minotaur. Diana was badly injured when the monster started to choke her, but she threw it against a tree. As Diana raised her sword above the Minotaur, ready to end its life, she realized that she could not kill the defenseless creature. Instead, she bound the Minotaur tightly with her Golden Lasso.

FACT

The Minotaur appears in Dante Alighieri's classic poem, *Inferno*. But the poet reversed the creature's famous features. Dante's Minotaur had a human head atop a bull's body.

Dante Alighieri

sacrifice—an offering, such as a person or treasure, given in exchange for peace with an enemy

SCYLLA

In the tales of Greek mythology, Scylla was a beautiful sea goddess. The sea god Glaucus fell in love with Scylla, and he asked the sorceress Circe to make a love potion. Circe was so jealous that she gave Scylla a potion that turned her into a fearsome monster with six heads. Filled with sorrow and anger, Scylla retreated to a cave on one side of the narrow channel that separated Italy from Sicily.

When the warrior Odysseus sailed too close to Scylla, she snatched up six crewmen in her hungry mouths and swallowed the sailors. The remaining sailors quickly escaped before she could come back for another meal.

In Wonder Woman's mythology, an ancient **deity** known as the Shattered God attempted to take control of the universe. He first turned the gods on Mount Olympus into statues. Then he took possession of many monsters, including Scylla, in an effort to destroy the Amazons. Even though Wonder Woman had temporarily lost her powers, she still managed to defeat Scylla by throwing her royal tiara at the beast. Her handy headgear severed all six of Scylla's heads.

deity—a god or goddess

MENACING MUSIC

Odysseus faced other seaside perils in addition to Scylla. Among the most dangerous were the sea-nymphs known as the Sirens. The bewitching songs of the Sirens were known to lure sailors to their deaths.

HARPIES

In Greek mythology, the harpies were horrible flying creatures with the faces of women and the bodies of vultures. These horrifying monsters tortured humans, made people disappear, and dragged mortal souls to the underworld. The harpies were sometimes sent by the gods to punish criminals, a task the harpies enjoyed because they loved torturing their **prey**. The harpies were always hungry. They never hesitated to use their sharp claws to steal food from their victims.

prey—an animal hunted by
another animal for food

The harpies also appeared in Roman mythology, notably when they attacked the Trojans. The mighty Trojan warriors settled in Italy and founded the Roman race.

Harpies have appeared in Wonder Woman's world several times. One of Princess Diana's closest friends on Themyscira was the Amazon known as Mala. One time, a horde of flying harpies attacked Mala. Without hesitation, Diana bravely jumped on top of the harpy that was holding Mala and freed her friend from the sharp claws of the beast.

During the War of the Gods, the evil witch Circe sent an army of ravenous harpies to attack Gotham City. Diana also battled harpies during the annual contest on Themyscira to determine whether she could continue to be Wonder Woman.

HARPY EAGLES

Harpy eagles live in the rain forests of Central and South America. Like the harpies of Greek mythology, they use their sharp claws to snatch up food. Their mealtime victims include monkeys, lizards, and sloths.

CHAPTER 3
Slithering Serpents

HYDRA

The nine-headed dragon-like creature known as the Hydra was one of the fiercest monsters in Greek mythology. It lived in the swamps of Lerna, a city in southern Greece.

When a Greek king ordered Hercules to perform 12 nearly impossible tasks, known as labors, one of his most difficult was to slay the Hydra. Each time Hercules sliced off one of the Hydra's heads, another two grew in its place to attack him. As a last resort, Hercules asked his nephew, Iolaus, to bring him a stick of burning wood. After Hercules cut off a head, he then burned the monster's neck so that a new head could not grow in its place.

The fire-breathing Hydra once attacked Wonder Woman when she journeyed to the pits of Tartarus. She used her Golden Lasso of Truth to bind together the creature's heads. She then shot an arrow into the Hydra's heart and killed the monster. Another Amazon named Artemis created deadly arrows by dipping them into the Hydra's blood, which was laced with **venom**.

Years later, the sorceress Circe created a new Hydra. Wonder Woman defeated that monster when it attacked the Greek embassy in Washington, D.C.

IT'S IN THE STARS

Mythological characters have inspired the names of many **constellations,** including Perseus, Pegasus, and Hercules. The serpent-shaped Hydra is the longest of the 88 constellations and also the largest in overall size. The Hydra constellation is so long that it takes more than six hours to rise into view each night.

Hydra constellation

venom—a poisonous liquid produced by some animals

constellation—a group of stars that forms a shape

QUETZALCOATL

The Aztecs ruled a mighty **empire** in Mexico during the 1400s and the early 1500s. In their mythology, the god Quetzalcoatl was the spirit of life. His name meant "winged serpent," and he was usually shown as a large feathered snake. Some believed that Quetzalcoatl created the human race by sprinkling blood on bones he brought back from the underworld. He also carried a small ball, which he playfully bounced to demonstrate the "game of life" to his followers.

In one story, the war god Tezcatlipoca tricked Quetzalcoatl into behaving badly. Quetzalcoatl was so ashamed of his actions that he built a funeral **pyre** and walked into its flames. His spirit soared into the sky and became the morning star. Each time the Aztecs gazed at the star, they dreamed of the day when Quetzalcoatl would return to claim his kingdom.

One of Wonder Woman's most dangerous enemies was Phobos, the Greek god of fear. He joined forces with the sorceress Circe and many of Diana's foes in the War of the Gods. Phobos revived Quetzalcoatl and tricked him into attacking the people of South America and setting fire to their forests. Eventually, Quetzalcoatl realized that he had been deceived. He turned himself into a rain shower to put out the fires.

empire—a large territory ruled by a powerful leader

pyre—a pile of wood built to burn a dead body for a funeral

THE RETURN OF QUETZALCOATL

Aztec legend predicted that Quetzalcoatl would return in Year One of the Aztec calendar (1519 in our calendar) and reclaim his kingdom. In a strange twist of fate, 1519 was the year that the Spanish conquistador Hernán Cortés arrived in Mexico. Cortés conquered and ultimately destroyed the Aztec empire.

Hernán Cortés

MEDUSA

Medusa was one of the three Gorgon sisters of Greek mythology. Although her two sisters were immortal, Medusa was mortal. Like her sisters, she had a monstrous appearance that included facial tusks, razor-sharp teeth, bronze claws, and scaly skin. Most horrifying of all, she had wriggling snakes instead of hair. Anyone who looked into Medusa's eyes immediately turned to stone.

Some say that Medusa was once a beautiful woman who misbehaved in the goddess Athena's temple. As a result, Athena punished Medusa by turning her into a monster.

When the Greek hero Perseus accepted a mission to kill Medusa, Athena offered to help him. Athena knew that Perseus would be turned to stone if he looked at Medusa. The goddess advised him to only look at the reflection of Medusa in his bronze shield. By avoiding her direct gaze, Perseus was able to swing his sword and behead the monster.

In Wonder Woman's world, the witch Circe brought Medusa back to life and encouraged her to attack the Amazon princess. Just one look into Medusa's eyes would have turned Wonder Woman to stone, but the Amazon princess shrewdly closed her eyes during the battle and used her **instincts** to fight the monster. Just as Medusa wrapped her tentacles around Wonder Woman in triumph, the Amazon princess dragged Medusa over the edge of a cliff. Wonder Woman grabbed onto a tree limb to save herself, and Medusa fell to her death.

FACT
Drawings of Gorgon faces can be found on ancient Greek graves and temples. They were placed there to keep away evil.

instinct—behavior that is natural rather than learned

LADON

The giant dragon Ladon was one of the largest monsters in Greek mythology. Ladon had 100 heads and was able to speak in many different voices. Ladon's mission was to protect the garden of Hesperides from intruders. He stood guard over the garden's most treasured possession: a tree belonging to Zeus that grew golden apples.

After Hercules temporarily lost his mind and killed his own children, a Greek king ordered him to perform 12 mighty labors as punishment. One of those labors was to steal golden apples from Zeus' tree. In one version of the legend, Hercules tricked the Greek god Atlas into stealing the apples for him. In another version of the story, Hercules performed the labor himself after reaching over the garden wall and firing an arrow that killed Ladon. The spirit of Ladon then traveled far above Earth and became the constellation Draco.

After thousands of years, Ladon was revived by the Amazons of Wonder Woman's world. He found a home within the Wonderdome, a giant crystal fortress floating high above the earth. Ladon lived there happily and became a valuable **ally** to Wonder Woman. He offered expert advice to the Amazon princess.

FACT

There are cultural differences in the way dragons have been portrayed over the years. European dragons tend to have wings. Asian dragons are often shown as large snakes.

ally—a person or country that helps and supports another

24

FOSSIL-FUELED MYTHOLOGY

Some historians believe that ancient discoveries of giant dinosaur bones may have led to dragon stories in mythology. During the 4th century BC, a Chinese historian named Chang Qu declared that a dinosaur fossil had to be the remains of a dragon.

CHAPTER 4
Tricksters and Riddlers

ANANSI

Tricksters are creatures in mythology that use **cunning** to fool others. Some tricksters are able to take the form of another creature. Doing so allows them to move easily between the human and animal worlds.

In African mythology, the trickster Anansi was a giant spider that could take a human form. He was so clever, he could outwit people, animals, and even gods. In some versions of the Anansi myths, he even helped to create the sun, moon, stars, and human beings. African slaves brought the tales of the trickster Anansi to America, but the name of the character was changed to Aunt Nancy.

Sometimes, tricksters use their skills to help others. One time, Anansi escaped from a burning brushfire by hiding in an antelope's ear and whispering the best escape route. Anansi then rewarded the antelope by weaving a giant web to protect her children from hungry lions.

In Wonder Woman's world, the villainous Doctor Psycho tortured a man named Richard Agoras and infected him with the deadly Pandora Virus. The virus changed Agoras into a giant deadly spider that terrorized the public. Wonder Woman joined forces with a blue-skinned warrior named Rama to cure Agoras. But she was unable to prevent Doctor Poison from releasing the virus as an airborne **plague**. Fortunately, the virus weakened in the air and lost its deadly effect.

BEWARE OF TRICKSTERS

Tricksters can be found in many lands. Native Americans told tales of the coyote trickster. When the coyote allowed the stars to escape, the Milky Way was created. The Tengu trickster in Japan was half-man and half-bird. He used martial arts to get his way. The Curupira trickster in Brazil was a tiny creature with backward feet. It would create tracks in the ground that were impossible to follow.

cunning—intelligent; sneaky, or clever at tricking people

plague—a very serious disease that spreads quickly to many people and often causes death

SPHINX

The Sphinx was a Greek mythological monster with the head of a woman and the body of a lion or a dog. Sometimes the Sphinx also had the tail of a serpent and the wings of an eagle.

The Sphinx loved to pose one riddle to those she met, with deadly results for her victims. She would ask, "What animal goes on four feet in the morning, on two at noon, and on three in the evening?" When people couldn't supply the correct answer, the Sphinx ate them!

The Greek king Oedipus solved the riddle when he replied, "Man, because he crawls as a baby, walks as an adult, and uses a walking stick in old age." The Sphinx was so embarrassed by his victory that she jumped off a cliff and broke her neck when she crashed into a jagged rock.

In Wonder Woman's world, the Sphinx of Greek mythology was brought back to life. It found a home within the Amazons' floating fortress known as the Wonderdome. Although the new Sphinx did not try to eat other creatures, it still often spoke in riddles, which sometimes annoyed Wonder Woman.

THE GREAT SPHINX AT GIZA

The Sphinx of Greek mythology shares only its name with Egypt's Great Sphinx. This giant statue was built at least 4,500 years ago in the desert near Giza. Archaeologists named it after the Greek Sphinx, but the Egyptian creature was male, with a **pharaoh's** head atop the body of a crouching lion. These features symbolized royal power. Its Egyptian name was Harmakhis, which meant "rising sun." Statues of it were placed outside many temples and pyramids.

CONCLUSION

Wonder Woman challenges the most dangerous monsters of mythology. From the heights of Mount Olympus to the depths of Hades, she battles shape-shifters, giants, and hideous beasts. Although these fearsome foes knock her down, she always bounces back. While she may be a princess, she's called the Amazing Amazon for good reason. Her adventures not only inspire wonderful tales of heroism. They also keep alive some of the most famous characters — monsters, villains, heroes, and gods — from classic mythology.

pharaoh—a king of ancient Egypt

GLOSSARY

ally (AL-eye)—a person or country that helps and supports another

banish (BAN-ish)—to send away forever

constellation (kahn-stuh-LAY-shuhn)—a group of stars that forms a shape

cunning (KUN-ing)—intelligent; sneaky, or clever at tricking people

deity (DEE-uh-tee)—a god or goddess

empire (EM-pire)—a large territory ruled by a powerful leader

immortal (i-MOR-tuhl)—someone who is able to live forever

instinct (IN-stingkt)—behavior that is natural rather than learned

lyre (LIRE)—a small, stringed, harplike instrument played mostly in ancient Egypt, Israel, and Greece

mortal (MOR-tuhl)—human, referring to a being who will eventually die

pharaoh (FAIR-oh)—a king of ancient Egypt

plague (PAYG)—a very serious disease that spreads quickly to many people and often causes death

prey (PRAY)—an animal hunted by another animal for food

pyre (PYER)—a pile of wood built to burn a dead body for a funeral

sacrifice (SAK-ruh-fisse)—an offering, such as a person or treasure, given in exchange for peace with an enemy

venom (VEN-uhm)—a poisonous liquid produced by some animals

READ MORE

Hayes, Amy. *Medusa and Pegasus.* Creatures of Fantasy. New York: Cavendish Square, 2016.

Hoena, Blake. *The 12 Labors of Hercules: A Graphic Retelling.* Ancient Myths. North Mankato, Minn.: Capstone Press, 2015.

Sautter, Aaron. *A Field Guide to Griffins, Unicorns, and Other Mythical Beasts.* Fantasy Field Guides. North Mankato, Minn.: Capstone Press, 2015.

Sherman, Patrice. *Legendary Creatures.* The Supernatural. Pittsburgh: Eldorado Ink, 2015.

INTERNET SITES

FactHound offers a safe, fun way to find Internet sites related to this book. All of the sites on FactHound have been researched by our staff.

Here's all you do:

Visit *www.facthound.com*

Type in this code: 9781515745839

 Check out projects, games and lots more at
www.capstonekids.com

INDEX